This book belongs to

....

The Strange Old House
and Other Stories

How this collection works

This *Biff, Chip and Kipper* collection is one of a series of four books at **Read with Oxford Stage 5**. It contains four stories: *The Strange Old House*, *Flood!*, *Princes in the Tower* and *Key Trouble*. These stories will help to broaden your child's wider reading experience. There are also fun activities to enjoy throughout the book.

How to use this book

Find a time to read with your child when they are not too tired and are happy to concentrate for about fifteen to twenty minutes, or longer if they are enjoying the story. Reading with your child should be a shared and enjoyable experience. It is best to choose just one of the stories for each session.

For each story, there are tips for reading the story together. At the end of each story you will find four 'Talk about the story' questions. These will help your child to think about what they have read, and to relate the story to their own experiences. The questions are followed by a fun activity.

Enjoy sharing the stories!

Contents

OXFORD

UNIVERSITY PRESS

Authors and illustrators

The Strange Old House written by Paul Shipton, illustrated by Nick Schon

Flood! written by Roderick Hunt, illustrated by Alex Brychta

Princes in the Tower written by Paul Shipton, illustrated by Nick Schon

Key Trouble written by Roderick Hunt, illustrated by Alex Brychta

OXFORD
UNIVERSITY PRESS

Great Clarendon Street, Oxford, OX2 6DP, United Kingdom

Oxford University Press is a department of the University
of Oxford. It furthers the University's objective of excellence
in research, scholarship, and education by publishing
worldwide. Oxford is a registered trade mark of Oxford
University Press in the UK and in certain other countries

British Library Cataloguing in Publication Data
Data available

ISBN: 978-0-19-276434-8

10 9 8 7 6

MIX
Paper from
responsible sources
FSC® C007785

Paper used in the production of this book is a natural, recyclable product
made from wood grown in sustainable forests. The manufacturing process
conforms to the environmental regulations of the country of origin.

Printed in Great Britain by Bell and Bain Ltd, Glasgow

Acknowledgements

Series Editor: Annemarie Young

Additional artwork by Nick Schon

Tips for reading *The Strange Old House*

Children learn best when reading is relaxed and enjoyable.

- Talk about the title and the picture on page 6. Then read the speech bubble.

- Discuss what you think the story might be about.

- Encourage your child to read as much of the story as they can.

- Give lots of praise as your child reads, and help them when necessary.

- If your child gets stuck on a word that is decodable, encourage them to say the sounds and then blend them together to read the word. Read the whole sentence again. Focus on the meaning.

- If the word is not decodable, or is still too tricky, just read the word for them, re-read the sentence and move on.

- Where you can, use voices for different characters. Encourage your child to do the same. Reading with expression is fun.

- When you've finished reading the story, talk about it with your child, using the 'Talk about the story' questions at the end. Then do the activity.

Children enjoy re-reading stories, and this helps to build their confidence.

Have fun!

For more activities, free eBooks and practical advice to help your child progress with reading visit **oxfordowl.co.uk**

The Strange Old House

What will the children find in the strange old house?

Wilf had come round to play.

"Wilma's got a netball match tomorrow, so my mum is taking me to Huntley Hall," he told Biff. "It's a stately home. Do you and Chip want to come, too?"

Biff was not sure. "Thanks, Wilf. But stately homes aren't very exciting, are they?"

"This one is!" said Wilf.

He pulled out a book from his bag. It was all about ghosts.

"Look," he said, turning to the right page. "It says here that once, a long time ago, someone actually saw ghosts at Huntley Hall!" Wilf grinned. "What if *we* saw a ghost there?"

Just then Chip came into the room.

"What's that about ghosts?" he said.

"Wilf thinks there might be ghosts at Huntley Hall," explained Biff. "But there are no such thing as ghosts, are there?"

Chip thought about this. "I don't *think* so," he said.

Just then, he noticed a familiar light in the corner. The magic key was glowing.

"I hope this doesn't mean we're going somewhere spooky," said Chip.

The magic took the children to the grounds of a big house at night.

"This place looks a *bit* spooky," said Chip.

"It's Huntley Hall!" said Wilf. "I recognise it from the picture."

"It's cold and windy out here," said Biff. "Should we see if anyone is in?"

Before she could knock on the front door, Wilf gave it a gentle push.

"It's open," he said. "Let's have a look around."

It was dark and quiet inside the house.

"Actually this place is *very* spooky," whispered Chip.

"Maybe that's why we're here," said Wilf. "So we can see the ghosts of Huntley Hall!"

"There's no such thing as ghosts," said Biff quietly. "I'm sure that . . ." She stopped. "Hold on. What's that noise?"

A soft scratching sound was coming from behind a closed door.

"What do you think is making that noise?" whispered Chip.

Biff held one finger to her lips as she went to the door. She reached for the handle and slowly turned it.

The children stepped into a large room lit by
oil lamps.

There was a piece of paper on the table and a chair
was pulled out, but there was no sign of anybody.

Chip picked up the paper on the table.

"It's a drawing of those flowers over there," he said.
"But who made it?"

"I know!" said Wilf. "A ghost must have done it!
The ghost of Huntley Hall!"

The children jumped when a voice said, "I am *not* a ghost!"

A boy stood up from a hiding place behind the desk. "*I* was sketching those flowers," he said.

The boy said his name was Henry.

"Why were you hiding behind the desk?" asked Biff.

"I heard a noise in the hall and got worried," Henry explained.

"I want to be an artist," he went on. "But my
father thinks that's silly. He gets cross when I sketch.
So I wait until everybody is asleep."

"You're a good artist, too," said Chip.

"I've got an idea," said Biff. "Why don't you sketch the three of us?"

Henry smiled. "That would be nice," he said.

Wilf put his hands on his hips and stuck his chin out. "How's this?" he joked.

Henry pointed to the fireplace.

"Perhaps you should just all stand over there,"
he said.

He took a fresh piece of paper and began to sketch.
Biff, Chip and Wilf concentrated hard on not moving
a muscle.

Suddenly a gust of wind blew through the open window. The curtains billowed and knocked one of the lamps over.

It fell onto a scrunched-up piece of paper.

"It's on fire!" cried Henry in alarm.

The other children turned to see the flame catch
at the bottom of the long curtain. There was no
way to put the fire out. It climbed quickly, growing
bigger and bigger.

"Quick!" said Biff. "We have to wake up
everybody in the house!"

The children ran to the hall and began to shout,
"Wake up! Fire!" at the top of their voices.

They heard footsteps clumping, and then a big
man in a nightshirt raced down the stairs.

"Where's the fire? What's going on, Henry?"
he demanded.

Henry pointed through the open door to the study.

Henry's father took a deep breath. Then he shouted in a booming voice, "Servants! We need water in the study right now!"

The children could hear more footsteps and shouts all around the house.

Moments later several servants appeared. They were carrying buckets, pans and anything else that would hold water.

When they threw the water onto the fire, it let out an angry-sounding hiss.

At last the fire was out.

"Who left a window open and an oil lamp lit?" asked Henry's father with a scowl.

"I believe you did, dear," said Henry's mother from the stairs.

It was only then that Henry's father noticed Biff, Chip and Wilf.

"Who are you three?" he demanded. "What are you doing here?"

Luckily the magic key had begun to glow in Biff's pocket.

Before they disappeared, Chip just had a chance to give Henry a final word of advice. "Don't give up art! You're really good!"

The last thing they saw was Henry smiling.

The next instant the three children were back in Biff's bedroom.

"It's a pity we didn't see any ghosts," said Wilf.

They all agreed that it had been an exciting adventure anyway.

The next day Biff and Chip went with Wilf and his mum to Huntley Hall.

Wilf's mum was happy to see how interested the three children were in the Hall's history.

The tour guide led them into the study.

"Two hundred years ago, a fire started in this room," the guide said. "It might have destroyed the house, but three mysterious strangers warned the Huntley family just in time."

"Nobody knew who they were, but it was lucky they were there," continued the guide. "Then they just vanished."

The children looked at each other in surprise.

"We didn't meet any ghosts," whispered Wilf. "I think we *were* the ghosts!"

In the next room, the tour guide talked about people who had lived in the house.

"Henry Huntley became a successful artist," she said. "Here's Henry's painting of his father, who claimed to be his biggest fan."

There were several of Henry's paintings and sketches in the room.

"Look at this one," said Wilf's mum. "It looks a bit like you three!"

The children just smiled, remembering the night when Henry drew their picture.

Talk about the story

Why does Henry do his sketching only when everyone is asleep?

Whose fault was the fire?

Why did Wilf say they were the ghosts?

If you visited an old house, what would interest you most?

Spot the difference

Find eight differences in the portraits of Henry Huntley.

Portrait A

Portrait B

Tips for reading *Flood!*

Children learn best when reading is relaxed and enjoyable.

- Talk about the title and the picture on page 42. Then read the speech bubble.

- Discuss what you think the story might be about.

- Encourage your child to read as much of the story as they can.

- Give lots of praise as your child reads, and help them when necessary.

- If your child gets stuck on a word that is decodable, encourage them to say the sounds and then blend them together to read the word. Read the whole sentence again. Focus on the meaning.

- If the word is not decodable, or is still too tricky, just read the word for them, re-read the sentence and move on.

- Where you can, use voices for different characters. Encourage your child to do the same. Reading with expression is fun.

- When you've finished reading the story, talk about it with your child, using the 'Talk about the story' questions at the end. Then do the activity.

Children enjoy re-reading stories, and this helps to build their confidence.

Have fun!

For more activities, free eBooks and practical advice to help your child progress with reading visit **oxfordowl.co.uk**

Flood!

It had been raining for days.

"All this rain," said Biff. "I wish it would stop."

"I'm taking Floppy for a walk," said Mum. "Who wants to come?"

Biff and Chip looked at her.

"Not us!" they said. "It's raining!"

In the end, Biff said she would go with Mum. They went into the park. It was not much fun in the rain.

"Look at Floppy," said Mum. "He can't help getting muddy. The ground is so wet and squelchy."

Biff and Mum walked across the park. They wanted to cross the little bridge, but the stream had flooded.

"I've never seen it this high," said Mum.

Biff was excited.

"Oh look!" she said. "The bridge is under water."

Biff began to wade across the bridge, but Mum called her back.

"It's not a good idea," said Mum. "The stream is flowing really fast and you can't see the edge of it. What if you slipped in?"

"If it goes on raining, the water will flood across the park," said Biff.

Mum looked thoughtful.

"I hope the rain stops," she said. "We don't want the flood to get as far as our house."

The next morning, when Biff and Chip were at school, it was still raining. The children couldn't go out to play.

"Another wet playtime," sighed Chip. "I wish it would stop raining."

"So do I," sighed Mrs May, too.

In the afternoon it stopped raining.

"Hooray! Now we can play football," said Wilf.

But there were big puddles on the field.

"I'm sorry," said Mrs May. "We can't play football today. The ground is too wet."

That evening Biff, Chip and Kipper were watching television. The weather forecast came on. Some bad storms were coming, with a lot more rain.

"Not more rain!" sighed Chip.

The storm came in the middle of the night. The rain beat on the roof of the house and it lashed against the windows. It was so loud that Biff and Chip couldn't sleep. Mum brought them a hot drink.

"Poor Floppy," said Biff. "He hates this."

In the morning, Dad took Floppy for a walk. Chip went with him. When they got to the park, Chip gasped. The park was flooded. It was like a giant lake. Chip thought the floods were fun.

Dad looked worried.

"I don't like the look of this," he said. "We don't want the water to get as far as our house."

Chip grinned at Dad.

"It couldn't go that far," he said. "Could it?"

But it didn't stop raining, and the floods grew worse. The water reached the edge of the park. Then it began to creep up the road. It came through the fence and flooded the end of the garden.

The road near Wilf and Wilma's house was flooded.
The children watched the cars going through the flood.
One car had broken down and was stuck in the middle.

That day, the school was closed. The hall was
flooded and there was no heating.

"What are we going to do all day?" asked Wilf.

"I'm sorry," said Mrs May. "We can't open the
school today."

When the children got home, they saw a lorry in the street. It was loaded with sandbags. People were taking the sandbags to their houses.

"We need you all to help," said Mum.

Biff and Chip helped to carry the sandbags. They were very heavy. Dad put them in front of the doors.

"I just hope the water doesn't come up this far," said Dad.

Mum looked upset.

"The floods may get worse," she said. "So there's only one thing to do."

She picked up a chair.

"We'll have to take things upstairs," said Mum.

They all began to carry things upstairs. It was hard work and Kipper began to get worried.

"What will happen if the water floods into my bedroom?" he asked.

"Don't worry," said Biff. "It won't."

Some things were too big and heavy to carry upstairs.

"What shall we do with the sofa?" asked Dad. Mum had a good idea. She got a folding table.

"We can put the sofa up on this," she said.

It rained in the night. Dad couldn't sleep. He was too worried about the flood. Then he heard the sound of water. He went downstairs and looked.

Oh no! The flood water had come in.

Everyone woke up. The lights didn't work, so Mum
lit a lamp. They all looked downstairs. The hall was
full of water.

"This is terrible," said Chip. "Lots of houses must
be flooded."

The next day, Biff, Chip and Kipper looked out of the window. The whole street was flooded.

"I can't believe it," said Kipper. "It looks like a river."

"It's amazing," said Biff.

A man paddled past in a canoe. It looked funny to
see a canoe in the street. The man shouted up to them.

"Are you all right?" he asked.

"Yes, thank you," Chip called back. "But we wish
the flood would go away."

Some fire officers came to the street. They wore big, long boots.

"Can we take you to somewhere warm and dry?" asked a fire officer.

"Yes please," said Mum. "I don't think we can stay here."

The fire officers brought a dinghy to the front
door. Everyone got in. Dad carried Floppy.

"I never thought we'd sail up our street in a boat,"
said Chip.

Wilf and Wilma were in their house. They were looking out of the window. Biff, Chip and Kipper waved at them.

"You can come and rescue us next," called Wilma.

A cat was stuck on a fence. The fire officer stopped the dinghy. Dad rescued it and gave it to Mum. Floppy looked at the cat, but he didn't even bark.

"He is being a good dog," said Kipper.

They went to a hall in the town. A lot of people were there. Wilf and Wilma came in with their mum and dad. Biff showed Wilma the rescued cat.

"Poor little thing," said Wilma.

"We may have to stay here tonight," said Wilf.
"We can't go back home to sleep."

Kipper was upset. There were too many people in
the hall. He didn't want to sleep there.

"I want to go home," he said.

Later in the day, Gran came to the hall.

"You can all stay with me until the flood goes down," she said.

The children were pleased.

"It will be fun staying with Gran," said Kipper. "Thank you Gran."

When the floods were over they went back home.
They gasped when they saw the house. The floors were
covered in mud.

"What a mess!" said Kipper. "I hate it."

"Never mind," said Dad. "Bad things like this happen sometimes."

He gave the children a big hug. Then he gave them some mops and brooms.

"And what's more important than all this mud? We are," said Mum.

74

Talk about the story

Why did the school close?

Why was Kipper upset in the hall?

At the end, why does Mum ask what's more important than all the mud?

How could you help if your house was flooded?

Odd piece out

Look at the picture closely. Which of the squares on the right isn't in the picture?

Tips for reading *Princes in the Tower*

Children learn best when reading is relaxed and enjoyable.

- Talk about the title and the picture on page 78. Then read the speech bubble.

- Discuss what you think the story might be about.

- Encourage your child to read as much of the story as they can.

- Give lots of praise as your child reads, and help them when necessary.

- If your child gets stuck on a word that is decodable, encourage them to say the sounds and then blend them together to read the word. Read the whole sentence again. Focus on the meaning.

- If the word is not decodable, or is still too tricky, just read the word for them, re-read the sentence and move on.

- Where you can, use voices for different characters. Encourage your child to do the same. Reading with expression is fun.

- When you've finished reading the story, talk about it with your child, using the 'Talk about the story' questions at the end. Then do the activity.

Children enjoy re-reading stories, and this helps to build their confidence.

Have fun!

For more activities, free eBooks and practical advice to help your child progress with reading visit **oxfordowl.co.uk**

Princes in the Tower

Can Biff and Wilma help the princes to escape from the tower?

"Do you want to come outside to play football with us?" asked Chip.

Biff shook her head. "No, thanks. I'm writing a story for homework."

"I'm going to help Biff with story ideas," said Wilma.

"What kind of story is it?" asked Wilf.

"I have to make up a new fairy tale," explained Biff.

"I know! You could write one where a brave knight rescues a princess from a tower," suggested Wilf.

Biff sighed. "Why is it never *princes* who need rescuing?" she asked.

The boys went outside to play. Biff and Wilma had fun talking about more ideas for Biff's story.

Suddenly the magic key began to glow. It was time for an adventure.

"What exciting place are we going to this time?" Biff wondered.

A moment later they found themselves staring at a
thick stone wall.

"Where are we?" Biff asked, looking around at a
gloomy room. There was not much furniture, only two
small beds and an old table.

Wilma tried to open the wooden door.

"It won't budge," she said.

Biff was puzzled. "Why has the magic brought us to a locked, empty room?" she asked.

Then a nervous voice from behind one of the beds said, "Who ... who are you?"

The room was locked, but it was *not* empty.

Two boys came out from their hiding place. The one who had spoken was around Wilma's age. The other was much younger, and he looked at the girls with wide, frightened eyes.

The girls told them their names.

"How did you get in here?" asked the older boy.

"Well . . ." Wilma began.

Before she could say more, there was the sound of heavy footsteps from the other side of the door. It was followed by the rattle of metal keys.

"Quick!" whispered the younger boy to Biff and Wilma. "Hide!"

The two girls ducked down behind one of the beds
just before the door opened. Two guards entered.

The shorter one set down a tray. "Here's some food
for the spoiled little princes," he said with a smirk.
The only thing on the tray was stale bread.

The taller guard scowled at the boys. "Your cousin
Edward is crowned king later today," he told them.

"So we've given you extra bread," added the first
guard. "To celebrate!"

The two boys sat in silence until the men left,
locking the door behind them.

Wilma and Biff stood up.

"What's going on?" asked Wilma. "Why are you locked up in this awful place?"

"I am Prince George and this is my brother, Harry." The older boy put an arm round his brother's shoulders. "We're here because our cousin Edward betrayed us."

"A few weeks ago the old king died," he said. "He was a good king, but he had no children. So who was going to be king next?"

Harry glanced up at his big brother. "The king's advisers looked at family charts and worked out that it should be George!" he said.

"A ship was sent to bring us to the city," continued
George. "But as soon as we arrived, Edward's men
captured us."

"Why?" asked Wilma.

"Because Edward wants to be king," said Harry. "So
he got George and me out of the way."

George nodded. "They brought us here and locked us up."

"I don't understand," said Biff. "Why isn't everybody looking for you?"

Harry was close to tears. "Edward told them that our ship sank in a storm. Everyone thinks we're lost at sea!"

George looked miserable. "Once Edward has been crowned today, it won't matter," he said. "As king, he'll be able to do whatever he wants."

"Then we'll just have to get you out of here today," said Biff firmly. She started checking the room's only window.

"It's no good," said George. "We might fit through the window, but it's too high to jump from."

"We're not going to jump," Biff replied, pointing at the beds. "First we need to twist those sheets into ropes."

Wilma pulled the sheets off the beds as Biff explained her plan.

Later the guards returned. Once again the door crashed open.

"We've got another lovely treat for you spoiled little princes," sneered the short guard. This time he was carrying only water.

His nasty smile vanished when he saw that the room was empty.

The tall guard looked at the window and the rope made from sheets.

"Oh no," he groaned. "They've escaped!"

The guards ran to the narrow window and peered out. Below them the knotted sheets dangled halfway down the side of the stone tower.

"What's Edward going to do when he finds out?" asked the short guard nervously.

"We'll just have to catch them and bring them back *before* he finds out," replied the taller one. "Let's get the other guards."

Without another word, they charged out through the door.

After the guards had left, the room was quiet.
Finally a voice from under one of the beds said, "I
think it's OK to come out now."

Biff and Wilma came out from under one bed, and
the two princes came out from under the other.

Wilma looked at the open door and grinned. "That was a great trick, Biff! Climbing down the rope would have been much too dangerous."

In the distance they heard the sound of bells.

"They're calling people to the crowning," said George. "There might still be time to stop it."

At the bottom of the tower, George pointed to a castle in the distance. "Edward will be crowned in the Great Hall," he explained. "Come on."

Wilma held him back. "Wait," she said. "The guards will be looking for you."

"That's true," said Biff. "Wilma and I will run straight to the Great Hall and delay the crowning. You two go the long way round. Stick to the quiet streets and make sure no one sees you."

"But how will you delay the crowning?" asked George.

"Leave that to us," grinned Wilma.

The girls had not gone very far when they passed a group of guards looking for the princes.

"Good thing George and Harry aren't with us," whispered Biff.

"Let's hope they make it to the Great Hall in time," said Wilma.

In the Great Hall, a crowd of lords and ladies had gathered to see Edward be crowned as king. Apart from Edward, nobody looked very happy about it.

"Do you promise to protect the kingdom and its people?" the Keeper of the Crown asked Edward.

"Yes, yes," answered Edward impatiently. Then under his breath he muttered, "Skip to the part where I become king!"

The Keeper of the Crown lifted the crown up, ready to place it on Edward's head.

"Stop!" rang out a voice from the back of the hall.

There was a gasp as all the lords and ladies turned to look at Biff and Wilma.

Biff pointed at Edward. "*He* can't become king. Prince George is *still alive*!"

Edward scowled. "Rubbish!" he shouted. "We all know that George is gone. Guards, arrest them!"

The guards did their best to catch them, but Wilma and Biff sprinted up a set of stone stairs and raced along a balcony.

They stopped when they saw a line of guards in front of them, too. They were trapped.

The girls glanced down at the doors and smiled.

"Your plan has failed, Edward," said Wilma.

Prince George was marching into the hall. Harry ran behind him.

"What's going on?" demanded the Keeper of the Crown.

"Edward lied to you all," George announced. "I am here to be crowned king." He no longer seemed like a frightened boy. He seemed like a future king.

Edward tried to run, but a couple of guards stopped him.

The girls came downstairs to the sound of
loud cheers.

George turned to them both and nodded gratefully.
"Thank you," he said. "You rescued us."

"You're welcome!" said Wilma with a big grin.

Harry was jumping up and down with excitement.

"Georgie!" he cried, tugging on his big brother's sleeve. "Can our new friends stay in the castle, too? Can they?"

Biff smiled. The magic key had already begun to glow.

"You'll be a good king, George," she said. Then the magic took them home.

Biff and Wilma had not been back in Biff's room very long before Chip and Wilf peeked round the door again.

"Have you finished your story yet?" asked Chip.

"Not quite," said Biff. "But I've got some great ideas for what to write about!"

Talk about the story

Why did Biff ask why it's never princes who need rescuing?

Why were the princes locked in the tower?

How did Biff and Wilma help the princes to escape?

Who would you like to rescue?

Where are they?

Find the things below in the picture.

a baby

a boy on a chair

a man in blue with a moustache

a dog barking

three mice

two people wearing baseball caps

a suit of armour

Tips for reading *Key Trouble*

Children learn best when reading is relaxed and enjoyable.

- Talk about the title and the picture on page 114. Then read the speech bubble.

- Discuss what you think the story might be about.

- Encourage your child to read as much of the story as they can.

- Give lots of praise as your child reads, and help them when necessary.

- If your child gets stuck on a word that is decodable, encourage them to say the sounds and then blend them together to read the word. Read the whole sentence again. Focus on the meaning.

- If the word is not decodable, or is still too tricky, just read the word for them, re-read the sentence and move on.

- Where you can, use voices for different characters. Encourage your child to do the same. Reading with expression is fun.

- When you've finished reading the story, talk about it with your child, using the 'Talk about the story' questions at the end. Then do the activity.

Children enjoy re-reading stories, and this helps to build their confidence.

Have fun!

For more activities, free eBooks and practical advice to help your child progress with reading visit **oxfordowl.co.uk**

Key Trouble

Can Kipper get out of trouble?

Gran had come to stay. She had presents for
the children. She had bought each of them a
Super Squirter.

"Oh no!" groaned Dad.

"A Super Squirter! That's brilliant!" said Chip.
"Thank you, Gran."

The children went outside to play with the
Super Squirters.

"Wait for me," called Gran.

Dad and Mum watched them.

"Just look at Gran!" sighed Dad. "It's like having
a naughty girl to stay."

Gran had a surprise for Mum and Dad. She had some photograph albums.

"What are these?" asked Dad.

"Old photographs," said Gran. "I thought you might like them."

"Old photographs of what?" asked Dad.

Some of the photographs were of Mum when she was a little girl.

"Look at Mum," said Biff. "She was quite pretty when she was little."

"And look at Gran," said Chip. "She was quite young once upon a time."

Biff and Chip went out to play. Gran showed Kipper some more photographs.

"Here I am when I was a little girl," said Gran.

"Why is everything grey coloured?" asked Kipper. "Was it all like that in those days?"

"No," laughed Gran, "only the photographs."

Kipper put the television on. There was an old film about two men moving a piano.

"That's funny," he thought. "They are grey coloured, too. They're just like Gran's old photographs."

The men made Kipper laugh.

At last, Kipper turned off the television. He went to find Biff, but she wasn't in her room.

Then Kipper saw that the magic key was glowing.

"Oh no!" he thought. "I'm all by myself!"

The magic took Kipper into a strange grey world.

"Everything is grey," thought Kipper. "This is just like the film I saw on television."

Two men were trying to move a piano. They didn't see Kipper.

"There is no colour," said Kipper. "I don't like all this grey. I want to go back home. This is a silly adventure."

He banged the key on the wall.

"Take me back," he said crossly. "Or put some colour in this adventure."

The men were still pushing the piano. They had to get it through a door.

"Come and help us," they called.

Kipper didn't want to, but he went across to help.

"We have to take the piano outside," said the big man.

"Then we have to lift it down some steps," said the little man.

"Now! We'll take the back," said the big man.

"And you take the front," said the little man.

"All right," said Kipper. He squeezed past the piano and got ready to help.

"When I call 'pull', you pull," said the big man.

"Pull!" he shouted.

Kipper tried to pull the piano. Suddenly it shot forward and slid down the steps.

Kipper grabbed the top and jumped on.

The piano ran down the street. It went faster and faster. Kipper hung on to the top.

"Now look what you've done," shouted the big man to the little man.

"It's not my fault," said the little man.

"I told you not to push so hard," said the big man.

Suddenly the piano came to a stop. It crashed into a hedge.

Kipper flew over the hedge and landed in a soft garden chair.

"Hey!" shouted the big man. "Look what you've done to our piano."

Kipper was cross. "This is a silly adventure," he shouted. "I hate it."

He took the magic key out of his pocket and banged it again.

"I don't like you," he yelled. "I want to go home."

Suddenly the magic key began to glow.

The magic took Kipper home. Kipper was pleased
the adventure was over.

But the adventure was not over. Something had
gone wrong!

Kipper was a grey colour. He looked like an old
photograph of himself.

Kipper did not notice this. He put down the magic key and went to find Biff and Chip.

They were in the garden with Gran. They all gasped when they saw Kipper.

"Oh!" said Biff. "Something's gone wrong. You look grey, like an old photograph."

At that moment Mum and Dad came out of
the house.

"This is terrible!" said Chip. "Do something to stop
them, Gran. They mustn't see Kipper."

"Leave it to me," said Gran. "You take Kipper inside."

Gran picked up a Super Squirter. She ran towards Mum and Dad.

"Gran!" shouted Mum. "Don't you dare. We're not in the mood for this."

"But I am!" laughed Gran. She began to squirt Mum with water.

Gran chased Mum and Dad round the garden.

Biff and Chip grabbed Kipper by the arms and took him inside.

"Good old Gran," said Biff. "Now let's get Kipper upstairs."

"Ouch! Stop it! What's wrong?" cried Kipper.

Kipper looked at himself in the mirror.

"It's the key," he said. "I didn't want to go on an adventure. Now the magic has gone wrong."

"What are we going to do?" asked Biff.

Kipper began to cry. "I don't want to look like an old photograph," he moaned.

Gran came upstairs.

"Mum and Dad are not too pleased with me. But I've made them a cup of tea," she said.

"You were great," said Chip.

"But what can we do?" asked Biff. "We can't let Mum and Dad find out about the magic key."

Chip had an idea. "Kipper's clothes look grey," he said. "Get him to change his clothes."

Kipper went to his room. He put on a red top.

"Oh no," said Chip. "Your top's turning grey. You still look like an old photograph."

Just then they heard Dad coming upstairs.

"Do something," hissed Biff. "We mustn't let Dad
see Kipper."

Gran grabbed some sheets from the beds.

"Pretend you're playing spooks," she said.

"It's dinner time in ten minutes," said Dad.

Dad went back downstairs. He looked cross.

"Oh dear!" said Mum. "What's the matter?"

"It's Gran," said Dad.

"Now what's she up to?" asked Mum.

"Playing spooks," said Dad. "Whatever will she get up to next?"

It was time for dinner. Gran and the children
came downstairs.

"Have you washed your hands?" asked Dad.

"And where's Kipper?" asked Mum.

"Well," said Biff. "We've made a little surprise
for you."

Kipper came into the room. Mum and Dad looked at him.

"Oh Kipper!" gasped Mum.

"Oh goodness me!" said Dad. "Is this your idea of a joke?"

"You look so … different," said Mum.

"What do you think?" said Biff. "Gran has made him look like a man in an old film."

"We love it when Gran comes to stay," said Chip. "Isn't she clever?"

"Er … yes," said Dad.

Mum frowned at Kipper. "Your mouth is a funny colour," she said. "Show me your tongue."

"Oh no!" whispered Chip. "His tongue is grey."

Kipper put out his tongue.

"Oh dear!" said Mum. "Look at your grey tongue. You must be ill. I'm calling the doctor."

After dinner, Mum sent Kipper upstairs.

"Put on your proper clothes," she said. "The doctor can see you in half an hour."

"Oh no!" said Biff. "Now Mum and Dad will find out about the magic key. Do something, Gran."

"I don't know what to do," said Gran.

Kipper went upstairs. Biff and Chip went with him. Kipper picked up the magic key.

"I'm sorry," said Kipper. "I didn't mean to be nasty to the key."

The key gave a little tiny glow. At that moment all Kipper's colour came back.

"I'm glad I don't have to go to the doctor," said
Kipper. "The magic worked just in time."

"I think it was always going to," said Biff.

"You mean it wouldn't have let Mum and Dad find
out?" said Chip.

"I don't think it would," said Biff. "Do you?"

Talk about the story

Why did Kipper get cross with the key?

How did Gran help the children to hide Kipper?

Why did the key give Kipper back his colour?

What makes you feel cross or impatient?

A maze

Follow the maze to get the piano to its destination.

Remembering the stories together

Encourage your child to remember and retell the stories in this book.
You could ask questions like these:

- Who are the characters?
- What happens at the beginning?
- What happens next?

- How does the story end?
- What was your favourite part? Why?

Story prompts

When talking to your child about the stories, you could use these more
detailed reminders to help them remember the exact sequence of events.
Turn the statements below into questions, so that your child can give you
the answers. For example, *Where does the magic key take the children? Who
turns out to be the 'ghost'?* And so on …

The Strange Old House

- The children are planning a visit to Huntley Hall when the magic key takes them back in time to the Hall.
- They think they hear ghosts, but it's just a boy who loves drawing.
- His father disapproves, so he draws in secret. He is drawing a picture when the curtains catch fire.

- They wake everyone up and they all put the fire out.
- The boy's father is cross, but the magic key takes the children back home.

Flood!

- It's raining so much that the family are worried their house will flood, so they take their things upstairs.
- Overnight, the house is flooded and they have to be rescued.

- They have to sleep in the town hall, but Gran saves the day and takes them to her house.

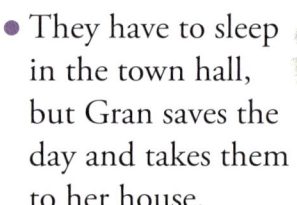

150

Princes in the Tower

- Biff has to make up a story and wants the girl to be the hero for a change.

- The magic key takes them on an adventure to a small, locked room in a tower.

- Two princes are imprisoned in the tower and the children help them plan an escape.

- They make it look like the princes have escaped through the window, but they're hiding under the beds.

- The children stop the coronation and tell everyone that the princes are still alive, but nobody believes them until the princes arrive.

- Now Biff has some great ideas for her story.

Key Trouble

- The magic key takes Kipper on an adventure on his own, into a black and white film.

- Kipper helps some men move a piano, but he lets it go and it rolls into a hedge.

- Kipper gets cross with the magic key and wants to go home.

- The key sends him home in black and white.

- His family try everything to bring his colour back, but nothing works.

- Only when Kipper apologises to the key does his colour return and he's normal again.

You could now encourage your child to create a 'story map' of each story, drawing and colouring all the key parts of them. This will help them to identify the main elements of the stories and learn to create their own stories.